LIFE DERAILED

A Divorced Mom's Survival Guide

For Balance and Healing after Divorce

Latachia Morrissette

Order this book online at www.trafford.com
or email orders@trafford.com

Most Trafford titles are also available at major online book retailers.

Printed in the United States of America.

ISBN: 978-1-4669-0197-1 (sc)
ISBN: 978-1-4669-0198-8 (hc)
ISBN: 978-1-4669-0199-5 (e)

Library of Congress Control Number: 2011919111

Trafford rev. 12/12/2011

www.trafford.com

North America & International
toll-free: 1 888 232 4444 (USA & Canada)
phone: 250 383 6864 • fax: 812 355 4082

Contents

Acknowledgements

I would like to first thank my Father God for the spirit of tenacity, wisdom, strength and the spirit of compassion. I give him all the glory in my success and prosperity in this journey we call life. I assure you most of my life I have ridden on the wings of angels.

My daughters Jaylise and Cierra, I love you more than I could ever explain on paper. You two give me power, courage and will to get up and face the world every day. You have helped to shape me as a person, because before you two I had no idea what I was really made of. Thank you for filling my life with many special moments. You two are my most precious miracles.

I would like to thank the Subscribers of Facebook Single Savvy Mom, LLC Fan page. You give me purpose and light each day, even when I am struggling. I am strengthened to be there and present for you. Thank you for your encouragement, feedback and support.

Thank you for all the Mocha love and support received by, Jennifer Reynolds, Bettina Vance-Johnson, Lainika Johnson Colbert, Donia Lawlis, Trisha Limiatta and Erica Alexander.

Thank you to Dr. Patricia Neff for polishing this manuscript into the precious gem that it is by proofing, editing and suggesting enhancements; In addition to her inspirational words of support for me, as an individual, and my mission to mentor and motivate women.

Thank you to my cousin, Shante Nix, for taking the time to look at the roughest draft of this book; taking it along on family vacations, and in between work and mommy life. All your feedback and encouragement has been very helpful. I love you along with your sincere optimism.

Dr. Will Moreland, you put me on track with the 16—week challenge. Because of you I am thankful every day for random encounters. You gave me the breath of encouragement I needed at that time to pursue what I had been putting off. You educated and inspired me on all the possibilities that lay after the birth of this book. Thank you!

I thank my sisters in Christ Thanette Burton for always asking me "Is the book done?" Always seeing the power in me I over looked; and reminding me how far I have come. Thanette you are my anchor, and one of my loudest cheerleaders. Chanda Teager you kick my butt with the truth, remind me of what I am made of and continue to challenge me to live up to it. You are a tough cookie, with a heart overflowing. I thank you both for never changing your position in my life as my friends. Moving me (literally) at my lowest moment of transition. I love you both.

Thank you to my loving family and friends who have supported me through one of the biggest transitions of my life. For listening to me cry, allowing me to fall without judgment and helping me up. Thank you for the encouragement and the praise.

Grandma Hoskins. I get my spirit of survival from the blood we share. You losing grandpa to death, after 18 years of marriage was difficult enough. Leaving you with 7 children to raise alone, simply takes the word difficult to a whole new level. I admire, respect and cherish you. If you can raise 7 alone I can certainly manage 2. You are amazing! Uncle Eddie and Aunt Ruth Hoskins, Aunt Regina Love thank you for acknowledging my progress as success, always listening and extending the hands of support.

To my amazing dad, Lennie, who chose to raise me as his own. I am the woman I am today because you taught me compassion, fairness and unconditional love. There is not a day that goes by I do not thank God for you being placed in my life and all you have done for me.

To Mamma Sam, you did not give me life but definitely allowed me to live it. Thank you for taking me under your wing and extending your role as mom in the absence of mines. I am always grateful.

Introduction

In my life I have had various difficulties, but none as painful as the ones that required adjustments; the recovery from having someone or something removed from your life. After a divorce, life not only changes, but the life as you know it disappears. I remember the day like it was yesterday. I was standing in front of my vision board attempting to re-create myself and to bring to fruition new dreams. I remember how alone I felt as all my friends, not all happy but married, could not walk me through this journey. And despite the good heart and will of my single friends they could never understand why I didn't just jump up, dust myself off and move on. They had not been a part of a union of choice with a person they loved and vowed, sacrificed and relinquished their personal dreams for. They loved me, both sets of friends, but they could not help me; I was in a place they could not reach.

I knew inside that I was now single in all definitions of the word; but why did I have to be alone? I felt no one understood me, nor could they console me. I knew I would have some level of support from my ex husband in parenting but how would I handle simple interactions with him? My heart knew I was discouraged yet brilliant and still beautiful underneath all this hurt and these tears. I also knew I would come through this, but how? What first? From that moment of thought I gave birth to this Survival Guide. God whispered to my spirit "Be strong, use your weakness as your strength and help others." I hope you enjoy this book and know it is prepared for you in love and understanding.

CHAPTER 1

What single means

As one unit, alone, unmarried

I am not sure what your understanding is, but it is basic. To be single means many things such as: standing on itself, one item, a thing, person not joining with another. It seems basic and it should be. However, single followed by mother automatically turns into partner. Wait! I did not do this so don't shoot the messenger.

Yes, I know they slipped it in somewhere, and I am not sure where. Somewhere between I do and I don't any longer there was an addendum to the contract that says "If there are little people between the two parties you must remain in contact in a civil manner as a partner." Yikes! I know and this sucks. For you mainly, but also for the children. This addendum protects the interest of the children; they need you both even if dad made a lousy husband let's hope he has the character to be a good father.

Many women often resort to holding the children hostage, projecting their pain and heartache on to them. Don't let this be you. As women, the natural nurturer, we often feel we have to protect our children from this awful man. Let's stop right here. There are some men who may not need or deserve access to their children. If there has been any abuse whatsoever that needs to be an issue that is not overlooked. Abuse includes alcohol or drug use, in addition to verbal, physical and sexual. In some of these cases dad may need supervised visits.

Let's talk about the majority. Most men, sane and of their right mind, need to interact with their children as often as possible. This is important to the development of the child. Many people say that children who come from broken homes do not excel, and I would like to disagree. You can still raise a successful, well-balanced child after a divorce. There are many women and men who can stand behind this. However, children that are victims to a broken heart seldom recover completely and often have many setbacks. What am I talking about? Well, when children lose one or both parents it ignites a grief that cannot be explained. When children grow up in a dysfunctional, unhappy home where the parents don't like each other, much less love each other, it causes damage as well. When a child is told something and the parent does not follow through, for example, the cancelling of a play date or weekend time with the other parent, the wounds will leave scars for a lifetime. This is what I mean by a broken heart.

Now, this is not going to be the easiest partnership because it usually starts with discord. However, as you heal and begin to grow from this experience it may be one of your most profitable partnerships in life.

Remember, single is not married, but that does not mean you are to raise your children alone.

Forfeiting a position

I've seen this and heard even scarier stories, where one party, usually the male, (but I am not here to judge) bails on their end of the deal by not keeping visitation or paying child support. Unfortunate as it may be, this puts you the single mother in a different race, and we will discuss this later on in the book. This lack of commitment from the other party will cause much heartache and make your position as single mother become as similar to that of a super hero.

So pick your cape in your best colors because you will wear it often, and make sure you have vitamin supplements and plenty of veggies because there will be lack of sleep resulting in fatigue and just a plain bad disposition. Understood, and you are justified, but this too will dissipate as you get your bearings and begin to heal.

Somebody Slap me, this must be a nightmare!

Journal Entry:

The beginning of the End, REALIZATION and SHOCK
Today I was angry, all 5 years flashed before my eyes, all miserable 5 and a total of 8 and I wondered why I stayed so long. My husband is out of the house and I just sit here and cry. I reflected on when he was here and I cry harder. Still frustrated and sad I wished so much for things to be different for a calming, a moment, just one moment of peace. I asked myself if it would have hurt this much, 3 years ago? Would it have hurt this much, 6 months ago? Why God? I love this man with every fiber of my being why can't I forgive him why can't I forget the hurt, why can't he love me the way I know I should be loved? Why did he not protect me as I expected a husband to protect his wife; as a husband should? I am frightened, God, what happens now? I do not want to be with someone who does not respect me, cherish and appreciate me. I want to be loved and valued for who I am not for who someone wants me to be.

I want for someone to look for the right in me and not point out the wrong, but have I done what I am asking? How do you live in a home treated as though you do not exist?
God, I need answers. I need to move forward, but for now I need you to help me get off this floor, I am lost and so very weak. Hold me God; get me up each day for myself and these children. Give me a blessing, a reason and a purpose. Please don't allow these years of my life to be in vain.

This has been a painful union for a long time, a selfish ambition, without life or love. Why am I still lying here expecting something different? I watched for years each stitch unravel and oftentimes would pull the strings myself. God, give me the strength to get up from here. I can't stop here. I can't!

CHAPTER 2

Progress/Shock

"One step at a Time"

"Never discourage anyone...who continually makes progress, no matter how slow." Plato

I remember waking up; I could feel each movement of my body. I rolled over and braced my hand on the nightstand. I pulled up supporting myself against the furniture. My feet were numb and tingling, each step resulted in the feeling of pins and needles. I opened my blinds and allowed just enough sun in to warm my face and my tears began to dry.

I couldn't move. I just stood there on pause with the warmth on my face, but it was progress from yesterday. Today, I am out of the bed. Well done.

Each day in the beginning of your new single mom life is going to be a challenge. I am not going to sugar-coat this for you, draw flowers or smiley faces. This is a place in your journey where it hurts and the regrets and second thoughts and anger still live inside of you. This is the beginning of healing, and as you know, all new wounds hurt. They need attention, a little alcohol to stop the growing infection and kill the bacteria, then some time to air out. Apply a bandage for protection so it can began the healing process.

Let's try not to tear the bandage off over and over again, reliving the pain of the past. Let's start by confessing and professing our hurt and anger. Stop saying you are ok. Seriously, it's ok to not be ok. Wait till the kids are away and SCREAM, cry and then get out a piece of paper and write it all down, random thoughts, fears, and ideas. Get it out, its ok, you have a right to be in this place. You cannot stay here long, the kids need a strong emotional and mental mommy so let's get thru this grief before too long; start purging now.

Pick up the phone and call your girlfriend, she has heard it before, but tell her you just have to get this out one last time and let it rip. Go through the house and put away all the triggers: old photos, gifts and mementos. If you cannot throw them away simply put them in a box and drive them over to a friend's garage for later. If you can move to a new home do so, a fresh start in a new place helps tremendously. If you have school age children this will be somewhat of an advantage. Take a few days off work take them to school and pull yourself together.

Each day, push yourself a bit further and do something you did not do yesterday. There are going to be days longer than others and that is understandable. Don't punish yourself for being human. Your whole life is changing right before your eyes; maybe you chose this and maybe you were blindsided, it is still changing. This is a metamorphosis stage. It is not a pretty place but it has to happen. The stretching and shedding of what you knew, the development skills you never knew you had will begin now. Somewhat like growing pains, this is a necessary evil. So many things in this moment of transition happen daily. Each day you will notice something different about yourself, you will do something you never thought you could, you will break through barriers, fears and false expectations. Progress will be happening each day.

Here are some activities that will help you get through the beginning.

1. Open the blinds
2. Take a walk
3. Take a bath with music you enjoy and just soak
4. Learn to meditate
5. Embrace a hobby, it is therapeutic
6. Stop reliving your story
7. Take a break from the chatter—Stop talking to your ex if it does not pertain to the children.

Stop Re-Living Your Story

During this initial stage of progression be easy on yourself. stop reenacting, reliving and retelling your story. Set a timeframe; start with 48 hours of no talking about this subject. This may seem like a long time right now, but then stretch it to 5 days and then 2 weeks. This is huge for you. You need to pick the people closest to you that you have told the dramatics of your divorce, they know every little secret, and they understand what really happened. Keep those people for conversations that allow you to vent. Select only a few. Why? Well everyone wants to know why you are not married anymore, what happened, who was she? They heard this or that. STOP IT!!! When people outside your select few ask about your current situation summarize it. Do not relive your story, do not start from chapter one and tell them every detail, making your mind, heart, and body go through this again and again. Come up with something short and to the point. Things didn't work out, and we are doing well." We saw life from two different places. Do not let people and their desire to be in THE KNOW, and your desire to purge, be heard or trash this man take over. STOP! Breathe and keep it simple so you can keep it moving. This time is all about you, the children, and your healing.

Court is in Session

You hear the gavel and the chatter in the background. When did it come to a court system telling you how to divide your personal items, protect this and share that? A place where the only time your voice is heard is in the ear of a highly paid negotiator and spokesman you have hired. How did we come down to dollars and days? When did a position take precedence over the welfare of the children?

This is a scary place, the court house. I find it cold and absent of logic, just full of reason and statutes, personal agendas and deadlines. This is where you land after many sleepless nights, paperwork, and parenting plans, plagued by night sweats and financial worry. This is where the judge, man or woman you have never met, looks at your life through their glasses and decides your fate.
Scary? Absolutely!

Many women tell me they could have done no worse without an attorney and others smile from ear to ear in satisfaction of the judgment they received from retaining one. Who do you use, can you afford them or should you go at this dissolution of marriage and child custody alone?

Each situation is different and many times people are too vested financially, emotionally, and mentally to sit across from their ex and draw x's and o's in the sand. In these cases a mediator and or an attorney could be best.

Do your due diligence in hiring an attorney

1. Let's NOT go with the cheapest because they are the cheapest
2. Let's look up their history in past cases
3. Have there been any infractions, loss of license or disciplinary issues?
4. How do they make you feel?
5. Are you heard and understood or rushed through a consultation?
6. Can you afford to retain and maintain them?
7. Take referrals from friends and family but still do your homework.
8. Is family law their expertise?

It is in the best interest of everyone that you are not getting food boxes in lieu of paying for an attorney. However, this is a huge issue that involves money, support, care for your child, assets, etc. Sometimes you just need an attorney and most are good at what they do. Other times there are document preparers, paralegals and public assistance programs to get you through this process. You will have to decide what is best for you. This is a stressful place and it is simply a must get through segment of divorce, you cannot skip this chapter.

Journal Entry

I look at my youngest child and wonder how she feels. No understanding of why her family is no longer one unit. No longer having any sort of stability; divided literally in half: half-truths and half-discipline; different structure and expectations. She can speak but has no voice like her older siblings. The courts often recommend weekly rotations. How confusing it must be in a little mind to take off my shoes here and run through the house carelessly there. How tiresome it must be to have a bedtime at 8pm here and 9:30pm there. How saddening it must be to be expected to remember the rules, the expectations, and routine as it changes every day or two. I cry, not because I hurt for me but for her. I cry because one child torn between two powerful forces (Mommy and Daddy). So torn that I question If I should step back and let him have more if it may hurt her less. Torn by the thought of her looking at me 10 years from now and asking why I did not fight for her or what I believed was right. How do you live with one foot on each side of the tracks? Carefully. I am overcompensating for things I cannot control, giving when not deserving and trying to pacify a child into a place of peace. A place as a mother I may never find because a child not at home in bed is always resulting in a mother with little rest or no peace. How will her stepmother treat her, will she accept her and love her in my absence? Am I regarded as mom and are my wishes respected in parenting? When my child calls for me, am I offered in comfort by phone call or visit or is the request looked over and denied?

Will this break my child into pieces that cannot be mended? What will come of this world of children torn between two homes; worshiping two Masters? I am saddened at the loss of control I have of the very life I created. God, I am going to need you more than ever this time.

More so with her than with me; tucking her in; reassuring and watching over. I won't know if any decision is right until it is made, I just pray it is not too altering for any of us.

CHAPTER 3

Flashbacks/Anger

They come many and often, brace your self.

I'll share.

I stood in the closet, head spinning, looking at the shoes I bought him for his birthday, the suit he wore at our last event together, and the sweaters I had picked for Christmas. My wedding dress tucked neatly in the back of the closet. I became dizzy, lightheaded and HOT very HOT I was and I began to snatch each item of clothing off the hangers, several at one time. I wasn't upset or angry I was full of RAGE and there was no coming back from this point. I grabbed a box and shoved each item, one at a time, into this box. Anything that reminded me of him, smelled like him I just tossed into this box. I began down our long hallway pushing this box and screaming things I don't even remember. I remember the pain, the loss, the stinging within my body; my soul was on fire. This was so unfamiliar to everything I had imagined, thought of and dreamed. WHY, WHY, WHY, What do I do now? I'm successful, attractive, a good mom, educated, so why me? What did I do to land in this ugly place, to deserve this? God, why are you overlooking me?

What do you do when you have done everything right, and it still goes wrong? I swing open the front door and kick the box on the front courtyard. You Asshole, Son of a Bitch, Ungrateful Bastard!! These things I remember, I shouted them so loudly they echoed in my head for hours. What must the neighbors have thought? I couldn't acknowledge anything but the pain I was feeling at that very moment.

I proceeded to the garage. I just threw things as I came in contact with them right to the ground with no regard, kicking anything at knee level. I couldn't see what I was doing because my eyes were so filled with tears, everything was blurry and distant and I was wet. A mixture of tears and perspiration I could feel the dampness against my skin, but the adrenaline was too much to contain.

I saw a picture frame, a collage type that had our wedding photos, baby 1st photos, vacation shots from the cruise and I just pushed it to the ground with all my strength and it shattered, much like me, into a million little pieces. Was I broken, would I ever recover? I can't move, paralyzed by fear and anger.

At this moment I felt a bit of relief and I sighed; I sat on the ground and did nothing. I sat in my tears and thought nothing for hours I was numb and on pause.

You have every right to be angry, and it is ok to be angry.
You will have frequent emotional mood swings. Bottled up feelings will explode and overflow everywhere and often. This is the stage where many send the text, email, or make that phone call to the "ex" and blow his head right off his shoulders.

Unfortunately, whoever is in the way is most likely to get the brunt of these emotions. Tread lightly because our children are standing nearby; watching and feeling your every move. You may have a short fuse, and find yourself easily agitated by the children. It is imperative that you get a break, rest often and take those impromptu bathroom stress relievers to get yourself together.

If you need help, get it. This is where your "Round em Up" list comes in handy. Do not be ashamed; you will need help; you will have bad days as you are only human. You never want to over-extend yourself and emotionally or physically hurt the children, so when you are angry please STEP AWAY and BREATHE.

Often children can understand if you say, "Mommy needs a few minutes. I'll be in my room for a minute." If you can't get away, find a movie you will all enjoy, play the quiet game and whoever talks first loses. Losing means bedtime or loss of privileges, but if you can grab a few quiet moments and keep the kids content that is a great option. Learn to use your anger constructively, try not to pick fights and blow up in public places. Many people take up working out, jogging, kickboxing or cleaning the house. Anger is normal, but proceed with caution; it is an extremely dangerous emotion.

Journal Entry

It has been a hurtful day, a day I wish never began. This is a day I wish I could take back, one that I could do differently.

Today I allowed him to anger me to take me to a point emotionally where there was no return. I can no longer allow him to say hurtful things to me, he is so mean, such a vindictive spirit I feel. He can have whatever he wants money, status, power, because they all seem more important than character and substance, family and sacrifice. I call, Mercy!

I've said mean things too God, please forgive me. I feel terrible after I say them, convicted I suppose. So many of those things I mean and I know they are hurtful. I know he is angry, frustrated and I feel helpless because he resents me so much instead of embracing me. God I ask that you allow me to be kind, allow me to forgive, allow me to heal and forgive myself. Lord, help me to be silent when I want to scream and strong when I want to give up.

God give me the strength to pick up my stuff. The stuff (dignity, pride, and heart) dry my eyes and move forward. Open the doors for me God so that I have the income to maintain a home for these children in such a dreadful economy.

I love you God, I am your child and I am sorry for my part in this. I don't want to hurt anymore; I am tired of fighting and crying. I'm tired of being over shadowed by anger, his or mines. Stop the madness. Wake me up from this miserable nightmare. Here is my heart Lord it is open to you.

Please bless our union, if we stand no more as husband and wife than as friends so we can raise the children we have been honored to raise. Please bless our children, allow them to overcome our mistakes.

Help me to continue to walk with grace, release me from this anger and rage. Lord, protect me from this angry and vindictive spirit that surrounds me, walking the hallways of my home.

Please guard my heart and soften his, forgive him too, for the error of his ways, he may have no idea what has been done.

CHAPTER 4

Days that Follow/The Covering

Denial

I do not remember much of the days that followed this. I did my routine quite normally but I did not feel a thing. I did not want to feel anything because the pain was unbearable. I did not answer my phone, watch television, or much of anything else. Every day was just me breathing and responding to what the kids may need at the moment.

Looking in the Mirror

I can't! This was the hardest thing for me to do but it is necessary. Your reflection is the truth, the vision of your pain and loss, the sight you cannot hide from. I never looked in the mirror, not for many months and I wore a wig that many people liked. However, the people who knew me never understood why I wore this wig. I am quite proud of my hair and had never covered it up for so long. This was not my efforts to recreate myself, to be a new DIVA or fashion statement. I wore that wig everyday so I did not have to look in the mirror. The wig allowed me to quickly get ready and not to have to stare in the mirror for very long. Hurtful? Yes, and very much so. I was in hiding, and under that wig was a tattered, scared, hurt and fragile spirit. My natural hair would show you that as it broke out in handfuls when I brushed it back into a bun. The wig allowed me to look polished and put together and I could be whoever I wanted to get through that day as long as I didn't have to look in the mirror at me.

Oftentimes we look past ourselves in the mirror never really looking into our own eyes. It is amazing how easy it is to look past yourself. It is real easy when you don't know who you are, when you do not recognize the person staring back at you. Denial, they call this stage of grief. This is a very painful stage and I want you to identify it. You must know that it exists in order to overcome it. The world knew I was separated, but my spirit and my heart had not yet accepted this truth. Are you in hiding, are you covered up?

There are so many ways to cover up the pain, the visual of self and reality. Some drink, smoke, sleep, prescription drugs, street drugs, over—eating and so many more covers we use. You cannot use this forever, you must come from under the cover. Maybe you are not ready today but you must come out.

Reality Check

Let's get this into perspective, you are transitioning. This is not where you will end up; this is not the end of your story. This painful place will not define you nor alter you in a way that you cannot come through it. Well, let me rewind. Unless you let it captivate, paralyze and hinder you, it won't.

I sat in my living room, tear stained face, and I told my girlfriend of many years. "I have nothing, absolutely nothing, I am at ground zero." She sat up, pulled her sweater together from either side and yelled at me "Nothing!" She startled me. "You have nothing! Let me take you downtown to the shelter and show you what nothing is! Let me show you someone without a home, food, clothing and you can compare what you have to nothing. Shut your mouth with that! You have everything you need.

What a pivotal point she made to me and with the authority I needed. My perception at the time was just that, a perception, my narrow one-sided perception. I was so down on myself that I could not see that I had everything I needed, right where I was, and so do you.

"When you are truthful with yourself, you start to see everything as it is, not the way you want to see it. The wounds in your emotional body are covered by the denial system. When you look at your wounds with the eyes of the truth you can finally heal those wounds."—Don Miguel Ruiz

CHAPTER 5
Round 'Em Up

Calling all troops, everyone! I mean mom and dad your in-laws, grandparents, best friends, god-mom, best friend #2, women from the mommy groups, cousins, playmates parents and so forth. Leave no person off this list and begin to see what and who makes sense to partner with. You need someone to get the kids when your meeting runs late and the traffic is awful. You need someone to take your child with theirs to boy-scouts and maybe someone to bring the other home from dance so you can put the baby to bed and clean up after dinner.

Woman, You need Help!

I am a proud and independent woman and mother but I only have two hands, and can only be in one place at a time. Really? I know we, as moms, wear capes and have an "S" on our chest in neon lights, but we didn't get the "twinkle of the nose" Jeanie skills where we can drop in anywhere at any time.

This will be the time when you see what your blanket of support is woven of. When you find out who your friends are and how far their : "Call me if you need me girl." really goes. If they offer help TAKE IT!

If they don't offer, ASK! Often people assume that if you're not in the fetal position crying then you are fine; and if you're not asking for help you don't need it. Both are furthest from the truth.

Learn to barter and barter well. If they pick up yours on Tuesday you can pick up theirs on Friday when you have a half a day. Or give them a date night, offering a free babysitting night for their help during the week. Look at it this way, your kids get playmates over and you repay the favor. Easy? Yes it is.

What if they don't want to help? No problem, move on. There is no one worse with your children then someone who doesn't want to be bothered with them. Keep it moving there are more people in the village.

You are going to need all participants so follow these easy must haves and get the Round up started. These are things to think of, write a name or two down that comes to mind after each subject.

1. Emergency Card
2. Late Pick Up
3. Extracurricular Activities
4. Sleep Overs
5. Tutors
6. Carpool
7. Emergency Sheets
8. Mommy Break (Do not Disregard)

What Mommy can do

There are several things and people you will need on this journey, but mom is going to need to round up support for herself too. Find local singles clubs, parenting groups and women's social events. As a mother and a woman you must have a supportive outlet. Round up your biggest cheerleaders, the people who support you and speak positive things into your life. It is important that everything you receive is positive, and this may mean you must start filtering. Mom needs to have a list too. Go down this list and find a person or a name or two that fits each category.

1. Girls Night Out
2. Vent/Cry Phone Calls
3. Share my Dreams
4. Support-They have been thru it and understand
5. Rescue 911 Can't Make it moments (Come Now!)
6. Boomerang (Why did I leave again? Bring you back to Reality)
7. Who am I?

Ship 'em Out

Now I know what I am about to suggest is not going to be easy, but at this point in your life it is non-negotiable. Round up the friends and family members that drain you, speak negatively and have nothing nice to say. Collect them all on a piece of paper and begin to remove them from your daily life. How? By any and all means necessary. Here is an option, in your cell phone you may have to put DO NOT ANSWER or BUZZ KILL as their contact name, so when they call you are quickly reminded of what they bring to the table (Negative Energy). If someone is hosting an event that brings you the blues, kindly decline. It is ok to be busy, not have a sitter or have prior plans. If they bring you down they must go. It may be family, and they don't go anywhere but you do not have to go where they are. Distance may be key at this moment in our life. There is no place in this transition for shackles, heckling, and just plain mean spirited comments. Ship em out fast, I promise you will feel better.

Journal Entry

The girls are gone for the weekend. It is so quiet in the house. There is so much to do but where do I start. For some reason I have no energy to do anything at this moment. I am thinking about what I would like to do, and still nothing, my mind is blank.

Who am I? What do I like and who am I outside of being a mommy and a wife? I wish someone kept notes on my life, and filed it away somewhere for reference. I feel like I have amnesia, is this normal? Why is it so quiet in here? I want to get up and maybe visit a friend but I would not make good company. I want to laugh but the tears always beat the smile to my face.

God, help me, what do I do now? I'll just lay here and marvel at the fact that I am still alive, for whatever it is worth I am here, and in that I will rest, I have done enough for today.

Goodnight

CHAPTER 6

Plan A, Plan B and to Hell with the Plan

I know as women and people in general there is an innate desire to be in control. To know how it will be done, when it will be done and have it all organized in alphabetical order with labels. The menu for dinner would be precise and all the food purchased on the Sunday to start the week. Laundry would be done and neatly put away, floors vacuumed, homework complete, wardrobe for the week picked out and pressed. Are you laughing yet? I am, because laughter keeps me sane. In addition, as I write this I think of the items I stepped over to get out of the house, the food I forgot to take out of the fridge and the laundry I left in the dryer. What is even funnier is that I don't care. I have let the urge to control and have perfection go. I have allowed myself to live in the house, watch a movie with the kids instead of folding the last load, go to bed before picking up and having a microwave dinner option on standby. I have decided to complete my to-do list and make lunch time at school with my daughter instead of mopping the floor and prepping dinner.

Life happens, and sometimes it is best that it does. It is great to have a plan, keep planning. Always have a backup as well, but sometimes chuck that plan out the window and make it happen, go with the flow. Some days just forget the calculated formula and mix everything in a salad bowl. My kids have had pancakes for dinner and non-matching socks on in the morning. Who cares! In the greatest moments of life just live, put the sock on and let's go already.

I love my kids, and they are unique in their own ways. The oldest is meticulous and refined. Her clothes are carefully chosen, everything is pressed and matching down to her sneakers. The youngest, I swear picks up whatever color attracts her, and sometimes they don't match, the top and bottom. She throws on boots with sweats and sneakers with a dress, and she makes it work. I don't fight this battle; I just let her be, because the beauty is in the fact that she can be freely her. That it is not planned but it works. Focus on the fact that it works.

Here are some "to Hell with the Plan" Tips.

1. Cook as little as possible. As a single mom you need two essentials in the kitchen. A microwave and a crock pot. This leaves just a little to clean up and makes cooking less time consuming.
2. Hire a cleaning service—If you can afford this luxury Get it! Once a week or once a month. I am telling you getting the dust off the ceiling fan, the baseboards cleaned, mirrors and windows washed without effort on your part is priceless.
3. Let the kids fend for themselves sometimes. Let them clean the hamster cage, feed the dog, water the plants and pick out their clothes for tomorrow. This teaches them some independence and teaches responsibility. Hey, mom cannot do it all.
4. Let them fold the laundry—so what if the corners of the towels don't line up.
5. Stay Prepared—This is everything from towels in the car for the unexpected mess, to an extra outfit, snacks, water bottles, napkins, baby wipes, lotion, toilet paper (I swear kids eat this stuff) etc. Be ready for almost anything.
6. Stop asking the kids what they want—and make the decision. I'm sorry but half the time kids don't know what they want, they don't have enough experience to know. Or they just

want the opposite of what the other wants for kicks and giggles. Here is a good example. I am at a restaurant and I ask the girls, "You want to try X" No! From one and a look of disgust from the other. However, once the food comes they want a taste and before I know it they have eaten my entire meal. Yikes!! If you ask burgers or tacos I promise they each want something different. Say, it's taco night! Sometimes just choose for them, they need that because they don't know, they think they do but at the end of the day, mommy knows best.

7. Get your Bearings—I tell you this with great tenacity, get it together. Get your space and time alone. You not only need it you deserve it. Have some alone time, and actually schedule it. Yes, I know, it sounds impossible. The essential word here is earlier in this paragraph. Planning! So I have prayer and meditation at 6am and every night before I sleep, but given a tantrum from an irate and very bossy 6 year old, mix it with a bit of 16 year old attitude and tie the bow of bills and life around it, I may say to Hell with the plan and lock myself in the bathroom for 15 minutes, or take a 30 minute walk. I have to keep myself together, the children need me to remain whole and sometimes I can't plan the breaks I need but I take them anyway.

There are No Instructions

I checked, I promise I did. I looked in the blanket, the car seat, behind her ears, on her bottom, under her arms, the bottoms of her feet and NOTHING!! No instructions. What the H E double hockey sticks! What do I do here? Now? With? When?

I am telling you much like the child itself; the journey has no road map, no instructions no highlighted chapters. We have to find our way and only the strong survive.

When my first daughter was born I just marveled at her from afar. I had no idea what to do with this precious breathing creature. It was so surreal, that I had just given life to something that now required nurture and care. I never had a green thumb so I was a little concerned. Every plant I touched had died so a human being was very overwhelming. I asked God to please watch me closely I didn't want to mess this one up.

To my surprise I winged it pretty well, and from the outside you would never know I was terrified and had no idea what I was going to do next.

I found divorce to be just as shaking. I marveled at the idea, I looked at my then husband and thought "What do I do Here? Now? With? When? How will I balance all this, I just learned how to be a wife now a single mother." The lesson book was way ahead of my learning curve. The rug snatched right from beneath me.

I have settled on the fact that this is a "learn as you go program", and there will be clues and hints along the way with no specific instructions. I planned to be married and grow old with this man. Have grand kids and burial plots next to one another. At worst, my plan B I thought, we may have our differences and arguments, or spending of money, mid-life crisis and we would go to counseling, but DIVORCE ouch, I did not expect nor plan this. Although I felt my hand was forced in choosing this. This cut me deep and I couldn't deny that. So to hell with it. There are no instructions even though the neighbors seems to have it all together and your friend from the mommy group is always giving you tips as if she wrote the marriage and child manual herself. Forget about it! You are not lost, you did not mess up the recipe there is not one. Don't dwell on what you missed, get your stuff together and let's keep it moving!

Now what?

Recreate you. Recreate the woman you are, and recreate the life you planned. You recreate you in every way. The images and thoughts you have about yourself and life must change. I hold on with both hands and embrace this roller coaster ride now, they won't let you off, believe me I asked. I wake up and face my fears, cry my tears, shake it off, stretch, grow and rediscover. I keep molding and sculpting these beautiful children I have had the privilege and honor to raise. I refuse to be a victim, I am victorious, I continue to rise and so will you.

CHAPTER 7

Reality vs. Fantasy

The Crossroads

It will be a calm day, and easy to remember. The day will be pretty and your spirit calm. The house may even be clean and dinner prepared when you get this call. The phone rings, and "I miss you" will come pulsating thru the phone line.

Hello? Hello?

Easy the conversation begins, simple and filled with awkward silences. What is this about? You will start to read behind the words that are not being said.

He will say he has been thinking. Oh my, good God, how do I get off this phone; you think. Say anything but . . . .

He says I love you, he says let's get over this and work things out.

Silence. Just air is shared between you two across the phone line.

You may rejoice in this or get nervous and blurt out "I gotta go!" No, this is not the time! Everything is just starting to make sense and you are not crying every minute of every day, it's up to once a week. You have managed to get on about your day without painful triggers and talk with your friends without breaking down. Now? You want to work things out now? Why? This should be your first question, and figure out the possible motives behind this call. Has his new love left, are the bills overwhelming, did he just get served from your attorney. You need to decipher if this is anything but sincere. You can't afford anything less.

There is nothing more frustrating in life than confusion. The Bible says, God is not the author of confusion. Here you are going on about your life, finally out of the bed, getting through a conversation without crying and here he comes with this craziness. Romanticizing our past. With the I'm sorry, she is not you, I didn't mean it, I'll do better speech. The nerve of this guy, really. You just wrapped you're mind around NOT being together and now he wants to work things out. Mmmmmmm.

This scenario could be reversed and you could want to work things out, because now you want to avoid this terrible thing from going any further. You have been on two horrific dates: one blind one that left you feeling like you had just walked into the twighlight zone. You went out with your girlfriends and no one asked you to dance. Last weekend you were stuck home; no plans nor invites. You want the tears to stop and the pain to go away immediately. You will want to bargain. "Let's make a deal!" You will have a conversation with the internal you and try to convince yourself that maybe it was not that bad, difficult and etc.

This is normal, you want to make a deal right now because the unknown is very large, real and scary. If he will just do or say the right things; If he would just apologize sincerely; change his attitude, I will go back to him. Many of these thoughts will go through your mind time and time again. Now is not a time for false hope, you have come too far. Identify this stage in your grief so you know what you are dealing with (a fleeting emotion) and how to overcome it and move forward.

THINK FIRST and then REACT

Everyone has the right to see if their marriage is going to work, to make sure that there is absolutely nothing left. I don't discourage reconciliation but I do say you proceed with caution. I advise a licensed professional counselor sit down with and go over where you have been, and what you may need to think about. Here are some interesting things to consider. You left, or were pushed out for a reason. Or they left for a reason. You did not get here on a whim and all things need to be reviewed, revisited and resolved. This is not a tennis match where we go back and forth with our lives or a game of CHANCE. This is your real life and you need to own every decision of it.

There is a sudden lapse in memory when we start skipping thru our past. Everything is romanticized. When our present circumstances are painful we suffer from dramatization of the past or selective memory. We choose only to remember that which was good, and conveniently forget that which was terrible. Suddenly the past seems so much bigger, better, and we are thinking of the good ole' days. We may feel desperate as though we'd do or give anything to go back to that time in our lives when our family was one unit.

Current events and maybe the holidays are just around the corner and you find yourself suddenly or still single. Now, you're wishing you were back together even though your ex-husband was mentally or physically abusive. We are *mentally tricked* into believing nonsense because it hurts right now in the present moment and we will do anything to escape it.

Let's be honest here. You are considering going back because the good parts of the relationship is all you focus on when the relationship is over. It has happened to several women that I know including myself. You are not crazy or alone in this thinking. If you know in your heart you have been to this rodeo one too many times; you know in your heart how it is going to end and that it hurts more than anything mentally or emotionally when with that other person, you may need to break permanently away from this situation. Stop second guessing yourself. When the anxiety creeps in, keep moving. Take the blows as they come, cry your tears and keep moving. It will pass. When the urge returns, Repeat! The day will come when you remember the pain and smile because you overcame it. You can do this. Do not be bullied and persuaded. Do not let him take up your time and visit as he pleases. Make him respect your time, space and decisions. First, you must respect them yourself.

CHAPTER 8

Do not JUMP right into a New Relationship

Emotional Accountability—Own You!

The one thing everyone is looking for after a break up is comfort;to be pacified in whatever way possible. Everyone wants someone to love, to hold and to make life look less scary. This is normal, and I still warn you that this is not the way to go. There are wounds you have now that you have not even noticed yet. Sometimes after a car accident you feel fine, walk away and shake it off. Later, a few weeks pass and your neck hurts or your back is stiff. Yes, damage has been done and you did not even know it. The next relationship has little or no hope for survival in most situations because you have not finished healing yourself yet.

It is really simple; take care of you first before you take on another. Your situation requires that you heal, and the children too, so you have big work ahead and another full-fledged all feet in relationship could lead to you smothering your pain, insecurities, and disappointments only for them to surface when you absolutely do not want them to.

Ladies, lets embrace ourselves for a minute, look inward and not outward. We are so quick to offer ourselves up emotionally and sometimes physically, and really do not have much to give. Save your energy, you need it.

When I separated from my husband I met the most endearing gentleman. Everything I thought I ever wanted in a husband. I left my married home on Friday and met this man the following Monday. Boooyah! Yeah, that quickly he walked into my life leaving me speechless. Educated, tall and handsome, he came in with his foot on the gas, to whisk me away from all of my worries; he extended a life of comfort among other things. I could not receive it. This short lived relationship collided with me becoming distant, and moody. I would sometimes project my anger and hurt on to this innocent bystander. Yes, very sad. I had to come clean. I had to do what no woman wants to ever do. Let this man go. I didn't want to and I had no conscious intention of doing such a thing. So I held on, and he recognized where I was. He brought it to me, that I wasn't ready and that all that was in store for him was a broken heart. Instead of the tears and the snappy comebacks this is what I wanted to say to him, this below is the truth.

Journal Entry

Dear Potential Suitor

I know you want to hold me, but your touch burns my skin. I am not ready to be held just yet.
I am not prepared to be loved. I am so far behind this wall that I cannot touch nor see you for who you really are, only for what I've witnessed in my past. How unfair it would be for you to pay the penalties for his actions. Timing they say is everything, and my friend this is a bad time. You, so perfect, you I prayed for. Me, not ready, I will hurt you in this. I know I cannot give to you what you may need or what you deserve. Let me go before you must forgive me for something I cannot help or explain.

What you need more than anything is time, and space to work through this. I am not telling you to be a nun. I know you are thinking, he is out dating and shaking his tail feather, what about me? I want to move on with my life too. You will, but let's move along properly, not to cause future heartache. Getting into a relationship right out of this one is equivalent to jumping into the flow of traffic; tragic, yes. Who cares what he is doing, it is all about you right now. Focus and be deliberate, taking one step at a time.

Suppressing the emotions
I am so numb, I can't feel the hurt and I don't want to.

Passion, sweat and orgasms. Reaching the height of ecstasy is the only objective. Touching, embracing, and taking all that is in front of you. Our bodies collide like perfect strangers in an accident on a rainy night. It happens so fast you can't remember a thing. Kissing your ear and licking you in places you did not know had reactors with such intensity. The sheets ruffled the air brisk, your mind absent from this entire experience. You want to break away but you can't. You want to protect your health, body and heart but you don't have the strength. So you lay there. So you call him knowing you have nothing in common, the relationship is going nowhere and that the goal is to remain numb.

So many women share with me their sexual escapades, several different men that are emotionally, mentally or legally not available; or one man alone that is neither of these things as well. Ladies begin to bury the hurt into the passions of the night, press them into the bed sheets of a stranger and then kiss him good night.

This emotional disconnect allows one to stay separate from their pain; an interest in only masking it with possibilities that only live in your imagination.
Intimacy without a connection is purely sex. You give of yourself freely to take away from everything you have lost and you begin to understand that the touch of this man or that man takes away from the hurt of another. For the moment that is, and only in that moment.
Value yourself and protect yourself from the unknown and the unworthy. This is a difficult walk and every woman has her vice. Many will fall in to the arms of another running blindly, oftentimes with intense ambition to loosen the grasp of another.

CHAPTER 9

Shut up already! One line will do.

If I have to hear this story one more time, I don't know what I might do. Are your friends saying this when they leave your company, is it difficult to get friends to answer the phone? Have you bored a date to death with the chronicles of your broken marriage? STOP!

How many times must we hear this story? Do you get some pleasure out of re visiting your hurts, disappointments and divorce? Guess what, no one else does either. There is a time and a place to grieve, but to heal you have to stop speaking this story over, and over, and over again into your present moments. Let it be. Listen, I want you to come up with a one liner. I want it to be brief and concise and to the point. It must be true but vague and I want you to then practice saying it every opportunity you get.

Ok, let me give you an example. I will use my experience. When I am asked, "So, what happened to your marriage?" Why is such a beautiful woman single? Did he cheat on you, abuse you, or what? Whoever let you go is crazy, tell me what happened. You are divorced, OH NO, girl what happened?

My answer is always the same. You ready for this?

Yes, I am divorced. Why? Well, it was a series of unfortunate events. I smile and walk away or change the subject. I told the truth and that is the end of my sharing.

Listen, I have a scar on my ankle from when I was 12, and when people ask me about it I say I was cut when I was 12. The End! They do not need to know I was cleaning the yard of the neighbor for extra money to buy a gift, and my brothers were there horse playing, and the weeds were so high, and it was so hot that I just wanted to get done. I was not paying attention and my ankle caught on to this old piece of metal and it ripped the skin down to the white meat, and they had to rush me to emergency, yadda yadda yadda. NO! Get my point?

Do not get me wrong, there is a time to share details. A prospect you may be dating does not need to know the details on the first few conversations or dates about your turbulent marriage, infidelities, money matters and etc. If he is around long enough you can find a time to share these things later.

The lady at the grocery store, bank or gym doesn't need to add your story to the gossip she has at the local coffee shop or mommy's group. This may be the best advice I give you amongst these pages, well, maybe not but it ranks high. Find your one liner that makes you feel content and honest and practice it. Then use it all the time, we are healing, remember.

Who did what? It is all in the Perspective

"The fact that an opinion has been widely held is no evidence whatever that it is not utterly absurd; indeed, in view of the silliness of the majority of mankind, a wide-spread belief is more likely to be foolish than sensible" Bertrand Russel

What do people ask, all the time, more than anything else when two people split? Whose fault was it? Huh? Really? Give me a break here, I am crushed and my entire life is upside down and you are asking ME whose fault is it? His, of course! Now take that same question to your ex, who is miserable, or dating, or paying child support on visitation and currently not the happiest. His answer, you of course! Maybe you had the affair, you may have had several and in your own defense you say he was a work-a-holic and not nurturing, non-affectionate or he had the affair, but he says you drove him away. So you say he is at fault. He may have had an affair, maybe several and he says you did not understand him, you gained too much weight, you were a prude or you had an affair first. It is a vicious cycle. Whose fault was it? What do your parents say, what do his parents say? What do your friends say? Honestly, at the end of the day. Whose fault is the divorce? Well, it depends on who is telling the story, right? Right! You cannot win this one, people are going to judge because they do; people will take sides because they do. Some will get it, others won't and I advise you, don't fight this battle. Whose fault was it? Depends on who is telling the story, it is their opinion and everyone has one, enough said. Use that as your one liner and I gave you this one. Any more questions?

People will always talk, you lived through this and it is your reality. Perception is your reality and unfortunately the other persons also. Next time someone asks you what happened and whose fault was it. Say kindly, "It depends on who's telling the story." or you can say, that is really none of your business, which it is not. Regardless of the road you take here on your response, shake it off and keep it moving.

"In all matters of opinion, our adversaries are insane." Oscar Wilde

CHAPTER 10
Things you Lost in the Fire

"It doesn't matter what your past looks like, you have a spotless future."
Melanie Gustafson

I am sure there are several things you could name that you no longer have; things of sentimental and emotional value. I am more than positive there was a trinket or two you admired and maybe even a car or piece of property. Before everything you know of disappeared up in smoke I am sure you had more than enough. The fact is without those things you still do.

The latter stages of grief include acceptance. It is taking what you have and making the best of it, with a smile.

"Do the best you can with what you have right now." Confucius

The most interesting thing is you came out of the fire, you and your children. Along with that your health, sound mind and the skills now learned to survive. You may have come out with more, not tangible things but core quality things.

You are shaking your head right now, saying yeah ok. Listen! You came out; you keep showing up every day for yourself and the children. You have learned to be strong; you have faced a fear of being alone. You are getting stronger with each breathe you take. You have the tenacity to want to get through this. You picked up this book, seeking an understanding a way a skill or tool. You are thriving, you are a success.

I remember crying one morning, angry at anything from the toy I just tripped over, the toilet paper on the roll backwards to the pimple trying to make its way to the top of my skin. I was allowing my emotions to flood my mind and upset me. I was letting the things that I had no control over control me. BREATHE, I said to myself just BREATHE.

In between breaths I allowed resentment to creep in. I hate dividing my time with my children, I can't stand seeing him smile in my face as the wounds to my heart are still bleeding. I lost this and that and more, I preach to myself.

Then my voice of reason spoke. SHUT UP! STOP THIS!

You cannot argue with what is, accept and be willing. Accept? Say what?

I don't want to accept this pain, loss and turmoil. However, if you do not it just stays there, stagnant and stinky; like curdled milk that condenses itself and permeates funk throughout your refrigerator. Let it go, BREATHE, accept this and move on, just like you accept the basic laws of gravity. Gravity—You jump you hit the ground. I use that one because no one can ever argue it.

I know you lost a lot in the fire, maybe more than yourself. However the things you need to rebuild, to move, and to prosper you still have. Embrace these things; cherish yourself and your children. Begin the love affair with yourself, love you like you want to be loved and you will exude the greatness within yourself. You're an amazing woman. You are a survivor; you will be on track and moving beyond where you were and even where you are today.

I have a sister that always kicks me in the butt lovingly. She reminds me of who I am, she has watched me from afar and when I lose sight, get distracted by stuff, or when I refuse to look in the mirror I look at her and she reminds me that I am not a victim but a victor. Let me be this mirror for you; let me remind you that this too shall pass, that you will overcome and that life has just begun. Evolve, Embrace and Enjoy!

"There are things that we never want to let go of, people we never want to leave behind. But keep in mind that letting go isn't the end of the world, it's the beginning of a new life." Anonymous

CHAPTER 11

TURN THE LIGHTS ON

Fighting Depression

This is the moment when everything becomes dull, meaningless and saddens you. This thing will keep you in bed; keep you from showering and maintaining yourself. This is a very scary place to be, and it needs your immediate attention. At this point of depression it has sunk in that you are in a very uncomfortable place, the sadness is undeniable here and everything is dark.

Want to get rid of stress, live life one moment at a time. Worrying about things that haven't happened, rationalizing why stupid people do senseless things, and brooding over your past will make you nutty as a fruitcake. If you get out of God's way, what was meant to curse you will bless you. Let go, trust God. by D Ivan Young

This may be the time that you need a professional, some do and others don't, really it depends on your overall health. It is important to find help when needed. You may need medication, meditation and/or prayer. Many need them all, and depression is hard to fight alone, so let's not try to do that.

Signs of depression include lethargy, tiredness, moodiness, a lack of interest in most things, mediocre work performance and you become easily agitated.

You need to stay surrounded by positive people, get a support group that you can connect with and try not to stay alone for long periods of time. Stay busy, and around family and friends as often as possible focusing on the reality that there is a light at the end of the tunnel. Even if you cannot see it, embrace the fact that it is there.

There are several things you can do daily that take the edge off.

1. Seek a Professional for Evaluation
2. Watch comedies (Laugh, Laugh and Laugh)
3. Get on the floor and play with your kids, their imaginations are endless
4. Get creative by painting, drawing, writing and sculpting
5. Journal what you are grateful for daily

These are all simple things and they are therapeutic. They keep your mind off the constant hold of negativity, sadness and hopelessness. If for any moment you think you are not needed, loved or appreciated look at your children. They need you, healthy, happy and whole. If you can't pull out of this dark place for any other reason let your children be the reason, let them be your light. Without you, their world would be empty and every day you stay depressed you give them a little less.

"Take one breath at a time, make one decision at a time, and focus on just the current day and what you can achieve. The saddest thing for a child is to be in your presence and you not really be there. Be in the moment, embrace them. You control more in life when you don't let the issues, things control you."
Latachia Morrissette

CHAPTER 12

Forgiveness is a Virtue

"To forgive is to set a prisoner free and discover that the prisoner was you."—Lewis B Smedes

For a long time I was angry at my ex-husband. I could not stand to hear his voice much less lay eyes on him. The very thought of him raised the hair on my back and my eye brows would burrow together, my heart would race and flashbacks went over in my head like a vivid slideshow on LCD television.

I remember what he was wearing when he said the most hurtful of things to me. I remember the look on his face right before I closed the door to leave for the final time. I remember the nonsense he said in counseling, on the phone, in our bed, to his relatives. Everything about him, I hated, simply put.

I would wake up in the morning and be angry at my life and again angry at him. It was a vicious cycle I could not break. Mad at him would equate to me being mad at the world and then I would implode and be mad at myself. It was horrible, hurtful and counterproductive. Every step I took and my hate for him would knock me back several yards.

Forgiveness is not automatic, it is a conscious decision, but it releases you. It takes the shackles off your legs and removes that cloud of darkness from around you; a cloud so dark that you can't see out or ahead.

Learn how to forgive. Let go a little more each day and find a place of peace.

You will know that forgiveness has begun when you recall those who hurt you and feel the power to wish them well. Lewis B. Smeded

Here are some great quotes on forgiveness, as it is a virtue. However, I believe it is one of the most challenging things you must do. Your healing can not proceed until you do this. Forgive

Quotes on Forgiveness

"When we forgive evil we do not excuse it, we do not tolerate it, we do not smother it. We look the evil full in the face, call it what it is, let its horror shock and stun and enrage us, and only then do we forgive it." Unknown

"When you hold resentment toward another, you are bound to that person or condition by an emotional link that is harder than steel. Forgiveness is the only way to dissolve that link and get free," Catherine Ponder

"To forgive is the highest, most beautiful form of love. In return you will receive untold peace and happiness." Robert Muller

"Sincere forgiveness isn't colored with expectations that the other person apologize or change. Don't worry whether or not they finally understand you. Love and release them. Life feeds back truth to people in its own way and time." Sara Paddison

Forgiving You

"You can't undo anything you've already done, but you can face up to it. You can tell the truth. You can seek forgiveness. And then let God do the rest." Thomas S. Salazar

I cannot stress to you how important this is going to be for you. The moment that you decide you are worthy of forgiveness is the moment you will understand how important these next steps are

So, you made some mistakes. So, you overlooked some things. You miss him and your life together. You could have done things differently, yes you could have said something else and so could he, but you did not and you are where you are, accept this place as what it is and forgive yourself. It is ok, to let it go, it is ok to throw it away, come to terms with it.

You may be overly concerned with forgiving him, your ex. Or worse waiting on something you could never control which is for him to forgive you. Stop this insanity.

Wrap your arms around yourself, shed your tears and let it go. Forgive yourself today.

Too soon? Ok, start tomorrow. Open up and start to release the pain. This will be the greatest act of love you do for yourself.

"Love yourself—accept yourself—forgive yourself—and be good to yourself, because without you the rest of us are without a source of many wonderful things." Leo F. Buscaglia

CHAPTER 13
Acceptance

TODAY THE SKY SEEMS BRIGHTER, MY SPIRIT LIGHTER AND MY WORRIES FEW.

This day started much like many others, shower, makeup, hair, breakfast and out the door to make the best of the blessing I was given. Today! No more tears now, I find laughter often and look for opportunities to get out, mingle and meet new people. When he calls no hives, or goose bumps, my eyebrows don't connect together as I frown. I am looking good and feeling great. No, we are not back together, I tell my friends and family as they ask me why I am so happy. No, he didn't get abducted by aliens. No, I have not found a new love nor have I won the lottery. I have found myself, and every reason for living my life out loud. I have simply accepted where I have been and where I am now. I find myself more beautiful, more powerful and it makes me proud of me. Where I once cried for many hours over my loss of life as I knew it, I now smile at the good times and at the fact that I am no longer hurting. I am no longer in a place of frustration and resentment. Wow! This place I am in is peaceful and without fault. My spirit rests in what is, and I am at peace with what is. I am not thrilled that I am here in this space, experiencing these pains. I understand by forgiving I am not justifying actions or allowing more hurt; I am merely accepting the current moment. I am raising my children alone after many years of sacrifice and time. I just find happiness in raising my children; happiness in the fact that they exist and the fact that I am healthy and able to provide for them.

Today, I look at things differently. It is all in one's perspective, right?

Life is beautiful on the other side of all that pain, and fear. The hurt subsides a bit more each day. Not all my days are great days but I am not mourning anymore. I am no longer trying to force a square peg into a round hole. I am no longer crying in the closet. I am not trying to mentally edit and reproduce a marriage that no longer exists. I have forgiven myself, and him. I know that life is better spent being happy and true to one's self. I want happiness for him and I pray he feels the same for me but I will not wait for him to forgive me. I know there is no us, except in the DNA that runs through the blood line of our children. I am ok, with this, I understand. It took me a while to get here, and I am at peace with my present reality. I have walked into the realm of acceptance. I have decided I am going to live right now in the present moment and waste not one more day in the past. I Thank God. I never thought I'd make it.

"Acceptance is not submission; it is acknowledgement of the facts of the situation. Then deciding what you're going to do about it."
Kathleen Casey

Necessary Steps to Acceptance:

Believe you will survive this

1. Stop your complaining!
2. Stop holding on to the story and the pain; stop being a victim
3. Allow Beauty and Light Inside yourself
4. Think and Act like your Child
5. Forgive yourself
6. Forgive him
7. Then take a deep breath and just let go

CHAPTER 14
Believe in Love Again

"How can you be looking for this great love affair if you have never been a part of the greatest love affair, which is a love affair with yourself? Learn to love you before expecting others to do what you are not willing to do. "Latachia Morrissette

I can remember it very vividly, my heartache. I know there was a moment that I did not believe in much. I was not sure I could catch my breath, I was sure that God had forgotten me and that there was no glimmer of light at the end of my tunnel. I remember that bleak and very scary space I resided in way back in the beginning stages of my transition. I was terrified. No one would ever love me, I would die alone I felt. The pain was so real when watching other couples walk hand in hand, express public affection and smile. This whole scene just made my skin crawl.

However, my heart kept beating to its own tune. Writing its own script and pumping blood thru my veins that would allow me to survive. My spirit whispered reassurance. Somewhere inside of me I know love exists. Somehow around all this darkness I know it is here and I need you to believe this very thing. This is the moment you challenge your faith. Do you believe in God even though you never laid eyes on him? Do you know the powers of the universe exist even though you just feel them and do not see them? Do you understand that this is something you must harness? You will need to believe that love exists to ever experience it. It is not going to be simple to jump out into the world with open arms. You have to get the willingness to jump.

Remember:

This is Merely a Chapter in your Life, not the end of your Story

Don't be discouraged that you have had negative relationships now or in the past. There is always the possibility of positive change occurring. If you open yourself to this possibility there is the opportunity for it to come into your life. But your heart must be open and your mind must be clear.

Dating Yourself

How can you expect someone else to love the very person you despise; YOU. The person you blame for every failure and criticize at every opportunity. Let's start by learning to love yourself, in a way that you would want another to love you. Start by learning you, taking time for you, and embracing all those things about yourself you never liked. What is it, your nose, lips, hips, boobs hang too low? Is it your smile or walk you hate? Stop this!!! Look in the mirror and learn to love that woman that stares back at you. Believe that she deserves to be loved, nurtured, and caressed.

There are several things we look for in our mate. Several things we want him to have, do, and be. However what do we want from ourselves. Do we really value who we are? Do you caress yourself gently, pamper yourself consistently? Do you date yourself? Don't laugh here, I am serious.

Run to the store and grab your favorite flowers, inhale the scent of them all the way to the counter. Grab a glass of wine, apple cider a martini. Begin to run a bath, with bubbles of course. Turn some music on and lock your door. Light a candle or two and submerge your body into the water slowly, make sure the flowers are in eyesight because they represent the beauty you admire. You need to rest and reflect.

Take yourself out to your favorite restaurant. Grab an old friend or relative to catch up with. You do not need a man to validate what you are doing. Do you, be you, own you!

Don't be afraid to Pamper Yourself

There is one thing that cannot be ignored if you are to succeed at evolving and transitioning into to this victorious woman. YOU! You need rest. You need to learn how to treat yourself like a princess. Pampering does not always consist of spending money. Here are some pampering tips.

- Long Bath with a Glass of Wine
- Turn on the Mood Music
- Put on lingerie and Body scents
- Light Candles in the room
- Buy yourself your favorite Flowers
- Buy yourself Red Roses (You Love You)
- Sleep in (put the cereal bowls and milk on the counter and sleep in 30 minutes)
- Go get a Pedicure or grab a large basin and soak your tootsies with the remote control in hand.
- Pick your favorite restaurant and go dine alone and journal

- Grab the cookbook and make yourself a gourmet meal.
- Take a long walk in the park
- Write 20 things you love about you
- Take a long drive to the beach or local tourist spot.

Prepare yourself mentally and emotionally for love to walk into your life. Get fancy, feel good and enjoy. There is nothing worse than having an opportunity that you are not prepared to take on.

I giggle like a school girl when I think of how happy I will be with my future mate. First one must be happy with oneself. It is the most practical of things for you to do right now.

Love exists. Start to identify it daily. The hugs from the kids, the just checking on you calls the surprise deeds for and about you.

CHAPTER 15

Who is this guy Mommy?

Dating with Children

Dating Basics

Wow, did you ever think you would be at this stage. Looking to make new connections and ready to move on. This is exciting but it comes with a lot of questions. Here are the top 2 women have asked me online.

When is a good time to start dating again?

When you are no longer crying at the drop of a hat, endlessly brow beating your ex, and you feel ready.

When should the kids meet the new guy?

Let's keep the kids out of this issue for a minute. They are important but you need to know who this man is first and is he worthy of your time, let alone the children's. Kids do not need a revolving door in their lives right now.

Make sure this man is who he says he is. Where does he work? Who are his friends and what is his story? Check out how he is with his own children. Is he an active part of their lives, does he pay child support and does he have a relationship with them? Does he flinch when you mention a background check or ask questions about his past? If he doesn't care and provide for his own children what good will he be in your child's life? This is not the rule, but really general good common sense.

He Passed!

He passed the test and it's time to meet the new guy. Here are some helpful tips to get through the introduction with the kids.

1. Have a talk with the kids before he arrives. Let them know what you expect of them, which should be no less than respect and an open mind to meet a new friend.
2. When you introduce the kids, keep it light. Meaning, do something fun together, especially if he has kids, or have him over for 60 minutes of interaction to see how everyone responds.
3. Make sure the kids understand they don't have to like him to respect him.
4. Be open and non-judgmental of their feelings. They need to feel heard in this process too. It may take them a bit longer to warm up than you anticipate.
5. No affection! I mean none. Come on, who is this guy, and he is kissing my mommy too. Stop it! Save this stuff for a future more established relationship. Keep boundaries. If he is a stand-up guy he will respect this and understand.
6. Do not over explain; introduce this as your friend (no uncle, future step daddy stuff).
7. No spending the night until things get established. Kids and their space need to be respected too. It is important that kids feel safe and you will need to gradually move forward. Keep sleep-overs for nights when the kids are at dads, it is easier for everyone.

CHAPTER 16

Never Settle

Dating after marriage can be difficult. Many women cut right to the chase and begin seeing herself in a wedding dress and picking out her new home before the end of the first date. Because you can be anxious to get normalcy back into your life you may overlook a few things. Take your time, use discretion. Always follow your gut. I have made several mistakes in my life, some blindsided but most trace back to not following my instincts.

Ask yourself some questions. Does this man have values, and can he share them with you? How much time does he invest in his work, children and family? If he does not care for his own what can he do for yours? Does he treat you with respect? All the time? Where has he been in life? How does he make his money? Has he left a path of destruction behind or do others regard him as a good guy? Everything that glitters is not gold. Ladies, ask the tough questions. Do you have a record? Do you love your mother? How did you grow up? What happened in your last relationship/marriage? Are you still married? Does he have a paper trail or did he magically appear? These things are necessary things that cannot be overlooked. This is about you and the children. You just came out of a turbulent situation yourself let's not walk into the Sequel of a disaster.

I know it has been a long journey, you are tired and lonely. Please Don't Settle! Attract a man in your life fit for you and the kids, you have been through enough. Keep going, believing and praying for a man that exceeds your expectations.

Ask yourself these questions.

1. Would I want my daughter, sister or mother dating this man? Do you feel safe?
2. When you introduce him can you tell the truth about his employment and marital status?
3. Is he honest? If you watch him cheat others he will certainly cheat you.
4. Is he inclusive? When he talks and makes plans does he ever consider the kids and your schedule? Does he ever include them without you asking or provoking?
5. Do you see him standing up? Mattress Mombo a few times a week just is not enough.
6. Does he take you out? Men value their money and spend on that which they value more.
7. Be real, you may be fooling everyone else but you have to live with this guy, make crazy adjustments and put your heart on the line; is he worth it?

CHAPTER 17
Time out for the Children

"A mother's arms are more comforting than anyone else's."
—Diana, Princess of Wales

Listen! You have been through something very traumatic, but so have your children. Some children see divorce as a nightmare, and it will take time for them to heal too. They have the two people they love, trust and admire, attacking each other verbally and trying to pull them in two different directions.

I know, as a parent you want to do the best for your children, so let's start with what you can do right now to ease the pain.

Keep Down Conflict!

Please do not talk negatively about your ex, he is their father. I am sure you have your opinions about him, but do not share them with your child. Remember that your ex is a part of this child mentally, emotionally and physically. The negative words can be projected on to the child or worse received by the child as a personal attack as well, since they are half dad. Children internalize conflict. Keep it Down!

Never, Ever ask them to Spy, Lie or Take sides

Acknowledge their feelings, they have them and you must take them into consideration.

Accommodate

If they ask for their father, make him available.
If they miss their father console them and again offer a phone call or arrange a brief visit.

If they want to talk about the divorce, talk to them

If they don't want to talk about the divorce, allow them to be silent with their thoughts letting them know you love them and you are open to talk when they are ready.

Watch your Mouth!

Your child should never hear you talking in detail about the divorce, custody and child support. These are grown up issues that a child cannot understand. Arguments between the two of you should never be done in front of the children, control yourself. You are the adult, remain the adult. Children do not make these decisions; they cannot fix the issues so that should not be a topic of conversation when a child is in the room or within earshot.

Healthy co-parenting will take time; this is a learned skill that will be mastered through trial and error. Be patient with yourself and your ex, but stay focused on the best interest of the child.

The child does not want to lose your love, but they don't want to lose the love of their father either.

When it comes to the kids, behave yourself, watch your mouth and take the high ground even when it hurts. Divorce is permanent but so is parenting. Keep the peace the best you can, and you will be giving your children a gift that is simply priceless: A gift of love and support instead of conflict and disdain.

Mommy and Me

Remember to keep the bond between you and the children. Make sure you take time away from the crazy world and have a date with the kids. Make it a day when you leave your thoughts, cell phone and worries somewhere else. Make it a day you plan that you can all look forward to. If your children's ages are far apart try to cater to the ages. Don't take for granted they know you love them tell them often and express it whenever possible. It is amazing how much quality time means to our little people. Besides, take it while you can, soon you won't be cool enough to hang out with them anyway

Resources

Housing

- CoAbode.com

Divorce Attorneys and Support

- Nolo.com
- DivorceHQ.com
- DivorceLinks.com
- DivorceDex.com
- Divorcesupport.com family-law.freeadvice.com/family-law/divorce_law/ divorceandwomen.com

Child Care

- childcareaware.org
- care.com
- naccrra.org/naccrra/
- childcare.gov

Child Support

- supportkids.com
- onlinedetective.com
- asginvestigations.com

Domestic Violence

- thehotline.org ncadv.org
- US 1-800-799-7233 (SAFE)
- Canada 800-363-9010

Financial Planning

- financialdivorceblog.com

Mediators and Counselors

- family-marriage-counseling.com
- www.thesmartdivorce.com

Medical Assistance and Support

- pparx.org (free and discounted medicine)
- patientadvocate.org (help resolve medical bills)
- covertheuninsured.org
- cms.hhs.gov

Youth Centers for Support

- Youth Centers and Programs:
- Big Brothers and Big Sisters
- Girl and Boy Scouts
- Girls and Boys Club

A Message from the Author

I hope this book has brought some comfort, answered some questions, made you smile and gave you some insight. I do not profess to be the "know it all" in research and psychological development during the transitions of divorce with kids. I, however, can do one better. I am and have been in the trenches with you. Hurting, healing, being a superwoman. I am ahead of many and not as far as some on my own journey. I asked God that my mistakes, heartache and experience not be in vain. If I can save you a step, a few tears or a bad day then I have done what I set out to do. There is no magic wand for healing and moving on with life. This is something we just have to do and make the best of it as we go. The goal is to go at it progressively, your kids deserve the best mommy you can be.

Divorce with children is going to be one of the biggest challenges in your life and you are carrying precious cargo. Please be mindful of your words and decisions. I request that you join us daily on www.facebook.com/singlesavvymom. Here I provide daily inspiration, jokes, relevant articles and a forum for women going through the same yucky stuff.

From one woman to another: keep moving, believing and knowing that this is not the end of your story, just a chapter or two. Don't seek to know all the answers just learn the lessons. Soon enough this will pass and I challenge you to help another woman through her transition.

"The most difficult time in life is not when no one understands you. It is when you fail to understand yourself." Author Unknown

See you on the other side.
Latachia

WorkSheets

It has been said that we do our best work when we study. Here is your homework. Writing things down, gives validity. When we express ourselves on paper we give a breath of life to our thoughts and dreams. Once the pen is in motion you will write thoughts, plans and dreams. You can escape the space you are in now and create the life you desire. Before you know it these things manifest themselves in your life.

Thoughts become things.

Words do also so make sure you speak wisely and stop the negative talk especially towards yourself.

"Don't let your past steal your present."
Cherralea Morgan

<u>Top Resource Sheet</u>

Name a minimum of 2 <u>people</u> for each task.

Emergency Card—Kids are sick and no one can reach you.

____

____

____

Late Pick Up—You just can't make it on time.

____

____

____

Support-Time to talk or be listened to.

____

____

____

Rescue 911—Mommy Break! Please come get the kids.

____

____

____

Boomerang—Reality Check When you forget the reasons.

___

___

___

Sleepovers/Playdates

___

___

___

Girls Night Out

___

___

___

Insight Support—They have been thru a divorce or separation

___

___

___

25 Things you LIKE about YOU?

1. ______________________________
2. ______________________________
3. ______________________________
4. ______________________________
5. ______________________________
6. ______________________________
7. ______________________________
8. ______________________________
9. ______________________________
10. ______________________________
11. ______________________________
12. ______________________________
13. ______________________________
14. ______________________________
15. ______________________________
16. ______________________________
17. ______________________________
18. ______________________________
19. ______________________________
20. ______________________________
21. ______________________________
22. ______________________________
23. ______________________________
24. ______________________________
25. ______________________________

Bucket List

What do you want to do before you kick the bucket?

1.

2.

3.

4.

5.

6.

7.

8.

9.

10.

Your Final Test Question.

What does your most desireable life look like now? Visualize what you want moving forward (don't hold back) write it down. Dream!

CPSIA information can be obtained at www.ICGtesting.com
Printed in the USA
BVOW021125170112

280752BV00001B/65/P